CURIOUS KIDS
NATURE JOURNAL

Curious Kids

NATURE JOURNAL

100 Ways to Explore the Outdoor Wonders of the Pacific Northwest

FIONA COHEN
Illustrated by **MARNI FYLLING**

little bigfoot
an imprint of sasquatch books
seattle, wa

Manufactured in China by C&C Offset Printing Co. Ltd.
Shenzhen, Guangdong Province, in September 2022

LITTLE BIGFOOT with colophon is a registered trademark
of Penguin Random House LLC

26 25 24 23 22   9 8 7 6 5 4 3 2 1

Editor: Christy Cox
Production editor: Bridget Sweet
Designer: Tony Ong

ISBN: 978-1-63217-384-3

Sasquatch Books
1325 Fourth Avenue, Suite 1025
Seattle, Washington 98101

SasquatchBooks.com

CONTENTS

INTRODUCTION

You are a nature explorer, and this is your journal.

Why have a journal? To keep a record of what you observe in the world.

Observing means more than just looking at something. It means using a combination of senses to take in what's in front of you. It means making measurements and asking questions about what you find. Questions like: How many? How big? Where was it going? What was it doing?

When you make a careful note of what you find with your senses and your measurements, you are using one of the most powerful tools ever invented for figuring out what is going on in the world: science. Scientists observe and they make sure to record what they actually find, even if it's not what they expected to find.

How You Use This Book Is Up to You

How you record your observations and what you choose to keep in this book is entirely up to you. You can write or draw your observations—or both! Or you can take pictures and glue them on the pages. You can use tape to attach leaves you find. Maybe there's a grown-up who can help you write things down. Or you might use a phone or a computer to take dictation for you, and then print out and glue your words here.

You may want to share your observations with professional scientists. Sometimes they rely on people like you. People who record and share their observations about nature with professional scientists are called "citizen scientists," and they help scientists answer important questions. Some entries have suggested citizen science projects that you could participate in, and there's additional information and a full list of projects on page 155 of the journal.

It's fun to express yourself, and when you record your experiences, you think about them more and understand them more. If you struggle with writing as I did when I was a kid, don't let it stop you from recording what you find.

Drawing Tips

The kind of drawings scientists who study nature make are different from what you might do to make a pretty picture. When they draw, they are showing the details they want to remember. It doesn't matter if the whole picture looks like anything you might recognize, just that the details are there.

One of the cool things about drawing is that it makes you concentrate on the thing you are observing, and when you concentrate, you notice more things about it.

You will make mistakes. Everybody does, and it's OK. You are not drawing to impress anyone, just to record what you noticed around you.

Some tricks to make drawing easier:

- Before you start, take a long look at the thing you are drawing, and decide what details are important to you.

- While looking at the thing, trace around it in the air with your finger. Then draw the shape on the paper.

- If you see a mistake, don't let it stop you. Keep going. You'll figure out how to fix it faster if you keep putting pencil to paper.

Tools for Exploration

Tools you should bring when you're exploring nature:

- This book. Don't worry about getting it dirty. It's supposed to be dirty. You should be proud of every smear.

- Pencils. They're better than pens; they write in the rain, and you can erase them. Bring a few in case you break one.

- A ruler.

- A small plastic container, in case you find something you want to hold in place so you can have a closer look.

Other useful tools:

- A magnifying glass or hand lens, to look at small things. You can use the magnification feature on a smartphone too.

- Binoculars, for looking at things far away. It takes some skill to use these. When you find something you want to see through binoculars, keep your eyes on it while bringing the binoculars up to your face. Don't look away! This is not that easy, and it takes everybody a few tries to learn how to do it, so don't give up. Seeing things that are far away up close is worth it.

- Field guides. This book has information about only some of the many living things around us. At the end of this journal, there's a list of good field guides that will give you a more complete view of different topics. You could bring one or two with you when you go out, or have them waiting at home for when you return with your observations.

One more tool we hope you need:

- A blank notebook, for when you run out of space in this journal to write about everything you discover.

Rules to Follow

As you go out and explore nature, you need to follow some rules:

1. Be safe and obey the rules of the trail.

2. Be careful with the living things you are looking at. Don't pick flowers. When you pick up a log or a rock, always put it back carefully when you are done. When you pick up an animal to look at it closely, be gentle and always put it back.

3. Take some time to stop and be quiet while you explore. When you do that you'll notice a lot more.

4. Don't worry about getting your hands dirty. There are a few living things that might sting you, but it's safe to touch most things you find in the wild. Just be sure to wash your hands before you eat.

Happy exploring!

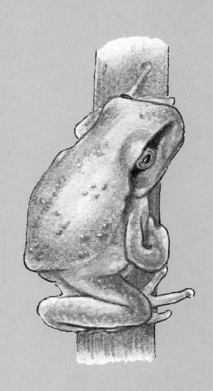

FOREST
AND
MEADOWS

In the woods in winter, groups of birds fly from tree to tree together in flocks. Chickadees often lead the way. They are sociable birds who call to each other as they move through the trees, looking for berries, seeds, and bugs.

Black-Capped Chickadee

I saw chickadees!

Date/Time: _____ **Location:** _____

What were they doing?_____

_____

_____

_____

What sounds did they make?_____

_____

Notes and Sketches

If you see a mixed flock of birds making its way through the winter woods, scan the trunks of trees. You might see one of these two birds, which like to eat insects and spiders they find in tree bark. Creepers tend to start their search near the bottom of the tree and make their way up while walking right-side up. Nuthatches start at the top of the tree and move downward while walking upside down.

I saw a nuthatch!

Date/Time: _____ **Location:** _____

I saw a creeper!

Date/Time: _____ **Location:** _____

What were they doing?_____

_____

_____

_____

What sounds did they make?_____

_____

Notes and Sketches

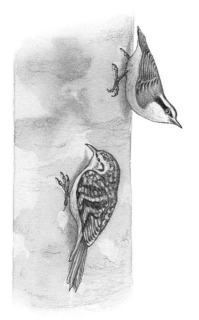

Red-Breasted Nuthatch (top)
Brown Creeper (bottom)

If you hear a repeating tapping sound on a tree or another object, take a look to see if it's a woodpecker. Five kinds of woodpeckers you might see are: the pileated woodpecker (the biggest), the northern flicker, the red-breasted sapsucker (which makes rows of tiny holes in tree bark), the hairy woodpecker, and the downy woodpecker (our smallest woodpecker).

FUN FACT: Woodpeckers have tongues that are longer than their heads. When woodpeckers are done feeding, their tongues coil back into their heads, around their brains.

I saw a woodpecker!

Date/Time: _____ **Location:** _____

What was it doing?_____

_____

_____

_____

What sounds did it make?_____

CHALLENGE: Look at a field guide. What kind of woodpecker was it?

_____

Sketch the hole or marks the woodpecker left on the tree.

Pileated Woodpecker

Notes and Sketches

Barred owls spread through the forest during winter in search of places to raise families. They can be in a fighting mood this time of year and can swoop at passing hikers. Sometimes they'll be out during the day. There are several other kinds of owls you might see, including great horned owls, western screech owls, and barn owls.

I saw an owl!

Date/Time: _____ **Location:** _____

What was it doing?_____

_____

_____

_____

What sounds did it make?_____

CHALLENGE: Check a field guide. What kind of owl was it?_____

_____

Notes and Sketches

Barred Owl

Owls eat small animals, such as mice and squirrels. They gobble them down whole, or in large chunks, and then afterward vomit up a pellet of bones and hair. If you find an owl in a tree, look around on the ground. If there's a lot of bird poop there, the owl likely goes there often and you have a good chance of finding an owl pellet.

If you want to find out what's inside an owl pellet, carefully carry it home. Get some latex gloves, tweezers, and a ruler. Spread out some paper towels and gently break apart the pellet on the paper towel. Use the tweezers to pick out each piece. Measure what you can.

(You don't need to find your own owl pellet to do this activity. You can find these online or in specialty stores. The owl pellets you buy are sanitized, so they are a lot cleaner than the ones you find on the ground.)

I found an owl pellet!

Date/Time: _____ **Location:** _____

Measure it. Length: _____ **Width:** _____

What did you find inside your owl pellet? Draw or write what you found.

Bald eagles build huge nests at the tops of tall trees, often with a view over water. They often come back to nests they used before. They add a little to the nest each year.

I saw an eagle's nest!

Date/Time: _____ **Location:** _____

How many eagles did you see?_____

What were the eagles doing?_____

_____

_____

_____

Draw the nest.

Bald Eagle

If the nest is somewhere you go often, use this space to keep notes and sketches about what you see each time you visit.

One of the first wild plants to bloom each year is osoberry, which some people call by its Latin name: *Oemleria cerasiformis*. It is a shrub with clusters of white flowers that bloom about the same time as its first leaves come out. You can find it in woods and parks.

I found osoberry blooms!

Date/Time: _____   **Location:** _____

What did the blossoms smell like?_____

What did they look like?_____

_____

Draw the flowers.

Osoberry Flower

Skunk cabbage blooms early in the year. Its big yellow flowers are stinky. They attract flies, which pollinate the plant. Skunk cabbage grows in swamps, so don't go too close, because you might sink in mud.

I saw skunk cabbage blooming!

Date/Time: _____   **Location:** _____

What did it smell like?_____

Draw the plant.

Skunk Cabbage

CITIZEN SCIENCE: Share your observations with scientists! Check out Project Budburst and PlantWatch citizen science projects on page 156.

Salmonberries become ripe in May and June. You can often find them at the edges of forests, and by trails and roads. A ripe salmonberry can be yellow, orange, dark red, or something in between.

NOTE: Not all berries are safe to eat. If you find berries of any kind when you are out exploring, be safe and don't eat them without approval from a trustworthy adult.

I found ripe salmonberries!

Date/Time: _____   Location: _____

CHALLENGE: Does each color taste different? It's hard to say. Can you create an experiment to find out? Share what you discovered here.

Salmonberries

CITIZEN SCIENCE: Share your observations with scientists! Check out Project Budburst and PlantWatch citizen science projects on page 156.

Stinging nettle grows in shady spaces in the woods. It thrives on ground that people have dug up, which means you can often find it next to roads and trails. Watch out for it!

Nettles are covered in hairs that are full of venom. When you brush against the hairs, they inject the venom, causing a painful and itchy rash. Most of the plant's stinging hairs are on the stems and under the leaves.

If a nettle stings you, treat the rash using an antihistamine cream. (One of the chemicals that makes nettle venom so itchy is histamine, a chemical your own body makes to keep you healthy.)

Although it hurts to touch stinging nettles, they are actually good to eat, but you have to cook them first to eliminate their sting. The leaves that emerge in spring are the best. Have a trustworthy adult help you pick them with gloves, steam them or fry them, and try them.

Stinging Nettle

I got a nettle sting!

Date/Time: _____ **Location:** _____

What happened with your rash?_____

I tried eating stinging nettle!

What did it taste like?_____

Would you eat it again?_____

Notes and Sketches

Black-tailed deer like to be at the edge of the forest, in woods near meadows or in meadows near woods. They will also browse among parks and lawns. You can sometimes find deer strolling around outside people's houses, even in cities.

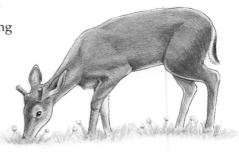

Black-Tailed Deer

Mother deer have fawns in late spring and early summer. For the first weeks of their lives, fawns lie still on the forest floor, and their mothers go away for hours at a time. If you find a fawn alone in the woods, don't worry. Its mother will return to take care of it.

I saw deer!

Date/Time: _____   **Location:** _____

What were they doing?_____

_____

_____

_____

Were there fawns?_____

How many?_____

Notes and Sketches

Fireweed grows in sunny meadows, roadsides, and places where there has been logging or forest fires. When it is blooming in summer, it attracts a lot of animals that drink its nectar, including bees, wasps, butterflies, flower flies, and hummingbirds. When they drink the nectar, many of these animals carry pollen from flower to flower. They are known as pollinators. Sit still next to a fireweed patch and observe what animals come by.

I observed a fireweed patch!

Date/Time: _____ **Location:** _____

What animals did you see?_____

_____

_____

_____

Fireweed

Notes and Sketches

CITIZEN SCIENCE: Share your observations with scientists! Check out the Bumble Bee Watch citizen science project on page 156.

The most common place to encounter a garter snake is a sunny spot by the side of a road or a trail. Snakes like to sun themselves. Chances are you won't notice a snake until it notices you and slithers out of your sight. Snakes have a scary reputation with some people, but there are no dangerous snakes living west of the Cascade Range or the British Columbia Coast Mountains. (East of the mountains, you might run into the Pacific rattlesnake, which is venomous.)

Western Terrestrial Garter Snake

If you pick up a garter snake, it will do its best to smear you with a nasty-smelling musk from a gland near the end of its tail, and it might bite, but the bite has no poison and may not even break your skin.

I saw a garter snake!

Date/Time: _____ **Location:** _____

What colors and markings did you see on it?_____

About how big was it?_____

What did you observe about it?_____

_____

_____

_____

As garter snakes grow, they shed their skins, and you can sometimes find snake skins in places where garter snakes often go.

I found a snake skin!

Date/Time: _____ **Location:** _____

Measure it. Length: _____ **Width at widest point:** _____

Use this space for notes and sketches. If you find a piece of snake skin, you can tape it here.

In the shade of the forest, western thatching ants build big mound-shaped nests out of needles, leaves, and whatever they find.

I found a western thatching ant nest!

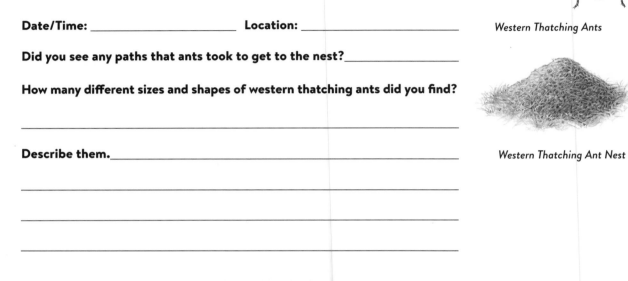

Western Thatching Ants

Date/Time: _____   **Location:** _____

Did you see any paths that ants took to get to the nest?_____

How many different sizes and shapes of western thatching ants did you find?

_____

Describe them._____

_____

_____

_____

Western Thatching Ant Nest

Draw the nest and try to include its entrances and the paths leading from it.

Take a close look at individual ants. Use this space for your notes and observations about what you see them doing and how they work together.

In wild forested areas, you can find banana slugs, especially after a rain.

I found a banana slug!

Banana Slug

Date/Time: _____ **Location:** _____

What was it doing?_____

_____

_____

If you get too close, it might react by shortening its body. Measure it. If

you wait long enough, it will stretch out again.

Shortened length: _____**Shortened width:** _____

Stretched length: _____**Stretched width:** _____

CHALLENGE: If you have a hand lens or a magnifying lens on a smartphone, see if you can take a close look at the four tentacles at its front. (Don't get too close, or the slug will retract its body.) The top, longer two tentacles are light sensitive at the ends, but they aren't just eyes; the slug uses these same tentacles to smell. The other two tentacles are for touch and taste.

Draw it.

If you pick up a yellow-spotted millipede, it will curl up and let off a gas that smells like almonds. The gas is cyanide, which is poisonous, but there isn't enough there to hurt you. (It is, however, one more good reason why you should wash your hands before you eat.)

Yellow-Spotted Millipede

I found a yellow-spotted millipede!

Date/Time: _____ **Location:** _____

What did it smell like?_____

What did you observe about it?_____

_____

_____

_____

Draw it.

Douglas fir trees have thick, rough bark. Their bark is so thick that sometimes forest fires burn the outside of the bark without ever harming the tree. When you are out on a forest hike, you can sometimes find Douglas fir trees with scorched black patches on their bark from when they survived forest fires.

I found a Douglas fir tree!

Date/Time: _____   **Location:** _____

Draw it.

Douglas Fir (left);
Western Red Cedar (right)

Western red cedars have gray-brown stringy bark. You might see an old cedar tree missing a strip of bark from its trunk. The bare spot will be at its widest at the bottom and taper to a point high above your head. That bare patch may be an area where Native Americans carefully peeled away the bark, which they use to make all kinds of things, including baskets, capes, and hats.

I found a cedar tree!

Date/Time: _____   **Location:** _____

Draw it.

When a dead tree lies on the forest floor, its decomposing trunk is a good place for young trees to grow. These dead trees are called "nurse logs." Sometimes you can't see the dead tree anymore, only a line of trees where the dead tree was.

I found a nurse log!

Date/Time: _____ **Location:** _____

How many young trees were growing on it?

_____

What else did you observe growing on it?

_____

_____

_____

_____

Notes and Sketches

Nurse Log

Douglas squirrels are very noisy. They chatter a lot. They love to eat the seeds from Douglas fir cones. The squirrels run up the tree and bite the cones so they fall down. They then collect the cones and peel the scales from the cones one by one, eating the seeds. If you find a pile of Douglas fir cone scales in the woods, that's the work of a Douglas squirrel.

Douglas Squirrel

I observed Douglas squirrels!

Date/Time: _____   **Location:** _____

How many squirrels did you see?_____

What were they doing?_____

_____

_____

_____

_____

_____

_____

I found a pile of Douglas fir cone scales!

Date/Time: _____   **Location:** _____

Measure it. Width of pile: _____   **Height of pile:** _____

Americans call this tree a madrone or a madrona, while Canadians call it arbutus. I am going to use both arbutus and madrone to describe the tree. Feel free to cross out whichever word you don't use.

Despite the word confusion, there's no mistaking this tree. Its bark peels constantly. The younger bark is smooth and green, while older bark is orange-brown and peeling at the edges. There are a few spots, such as near the base of the trunk, that have scaly gray-brown bark that doesn't peel.

I found a madrone/arbutus tree!

Date/Time: _____ **Location:** _____

What did you observe about the tree?_____

_____

_____

Tape a piece of bark here.

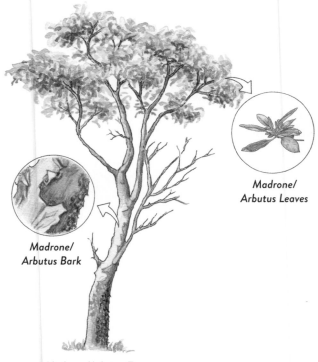

Madrone/ Arbutus Bark

Madrone/ Arbutus Leaves

Madrone/Arbutus Tree

Although madrone/arbutus trees have oval leaves rather than needles, they are evergreen trees. Instead of shedding all their leaves in fall, like maple or oak trees do, they shed a few leaves year-round.

I found a fallen madrone/arbutus leaf!

Date/Time: _____ **Location:** _____

Fallen madrone/arbutus leaves usually have several colors on them. What

colors did you find?_____

_____

Draw or tape the leaf here.

Near sunset on evenings at the end of summer, hundreds of Pacific dampwood termites crawl out of dead trees and take flight, looking for mates and dead trees to raise a family in. The closer you are to a forest, the more of these you'll see on summer evenings.

I saw Pacific dampwood termites in flight!

Pacific Dampwood Termite

Date/Time: _____   **Location:** _____

How many termites did you see? _____

What directions were they flying in? _____

Did you see any birds or bats eating the termites? _____

If yes, what did you observe? _____

_____

_____

_____

Notes and Sketches

Sierra dome spiders weave complicated webs that form domes on the inside. You can find them hanging on trees and shrubs in the forest. The spider who built the web usually sits upside down in the top of the dome. They are easiest to notice in late summer and early fall, when their webs are at their largest. That's the same time of year when male Sierra dome spiders visit females in their webs. So you might find two spiders in the dome, or you might find one spider in the dome and another spider at the edge of the web. Look closely!

Sierra Dome Spider with Web

I found a Sierra dome spiderweb!

Date/Time: _____ **Location:** _____

Did you find the spider?_____

Was there another spider?_____

Draw it. Show the shape of the web, and label where you found the spiders.

Big-leaf maples are common in our woods. They have huge leaves that turn bright yellow in the fall.

I found a big-leaf maple leaf!

Date/Time: _____ **Location:** _____

Big-Leaf Maple Leaf

I found a big-leaf maple leaf turned yellow for fall!

Date/Time: _____ **Location:** _____

I found a big-leaf maple bud opening in spring!

Date/Time: _____ **Location:** _____

Measure the biggest leaf you can find. Length: _____ **Width:** _____

Notes and Sketches

CITIZEN SCIENCE: Share your observations with scientists! Check out the Project Budburst and PlantWatch citizen science projects on page 156.

Big-leaf maples drop their seeds in fall. Each seed has a wing on it, and when you drop one, the seed will whirl around like a helicopter.

I found big-leaf maple seeds!

Date/Time: _____ **Location:** _____

Here's an experiment you can do if you have a tape measure. Pick up some maple seeds. Stand in one spot and then throw them all at once. Measure how far they travel. Distance traveled: _____

What did you observe about how they flew? _____

_____

_____

_____

Draw them.

Older big-leaf maples have a lot of plants and other living things on them. A plant or another living thing that grows attached to a tree is called an "epiphyte." Among the epiphytes you will find on big-leaf maple branches are mosses, lichens, fungi, and ferns.

I found an old big-leaf maple covered in epiphytes!

Date/Time: _____ **Location:** _____

How many kinds of epiphytes did you see growing on the tree?_____

Compare what you saw growing on different parts of the tree. What did

you see growing on the smaller branches?_____

_____

_____

_____

What did you see growing on the larger branches?_____

_____

_____

_____

What did you see growing on the trunk?_____

_____

_____

_____

If there was a dead part of the tree, what was growing there?_____

_____

_____

Licorice ferns can grow anywhere that has thick mats of moss. So you can find them on the ground, on rocks, or on trees in forests. In the summer, when it is dry, licorice ferns often die off, but they grow again when it starts raining in the fall.

Licorice ferns get their name because their root, or rhizome, tastes of licorice. Try one! Pull up one licorice fern, take it home, clean the root so there is no dirt on it, and taste a piece.

Note: Not all plants are safe to eat. Be safe and don't eat a plant you find without approval from a trustworthy adult.

Licorice Fern

I found licorice ferns!

Date/Time: _____   **Location:** _____

What was it growing on?_____

I tasted licorice root!

What did it taste like?_____

Notes and Sketches

A few days after the first big rains of fall, mushrooms pop up on the forest floor and in peoples' yards. Take a walk and look for some.

Don't ever put any part of a wild mushroom in your mouth. (Only mushroom experts know how to tell for sure which ones are the poisonous ones). But it is fine to handle them or smell them.

Coral Mushroom   *Questionable Stropharia*

I found mushrooms!

Date/Time: _____ **Location:** _____

How many kinds of mushrooms did you find?_____

MUSHROOM 1   **Sketch:**

Shape: _____

Colors: _____

Height: _____ **Width:** _____

Notes: _____

_____

_____

MUSHROOM 2   **Sketch:**

Shape: _____

Colors: _____

Height: _____ **Width:** _____

Notes: _____

_____

_____

MUSHROOM 3

Shape: _____

Colors: _____

Height: _____ **Width:** _____

Notes: _____

_____

_____

Sketch:

MUSHROOM 4

Shape: _____

Colors: _____

Height: _____ **Width:** _____

Notes: _____

_____

_____

Sketch:

MUSHROOM 5

Shape: _____

Colors: _____

Height: _____ **Width:** _____

Notes: _____

_____

_____

Sketch:

Use these pages for your notes, drawings, and observations.

BEACH

Ospreys eat fish. They hover over the water, and then dive down with a splash. Sometimes they catch a fish. Often they miss.

I watched an osprey fishing!

Date/Time: _____ **Location:** _____

How many times did it try?_____

Did it catch a fish?_____

What else did you observe?_____

_____

_____

_____

Osprey

Ospreys arrive back in the spring after spending the winter in warm places. Soon after they arrive, they will either build a new nest or spruce up an old one. They like to nest near the sea, rivers, and lakes, and they nest in trees and other high places, such as bridges, poles, platforms, and signs.

I saw an osprey nest!

Date/Time: _____ **Location:** _____

How many ospreys did you see?_____

What were they doing?_____

_____

_____

_____

What sounds did they make?_____

_____

If the nest is somewhere you go often, use this space to keep notes of what you see each time you visit.

Clams thrive on wide areas of sand or mud at low tide. If you go to a beach like that, you may find a lot of clamshells on the beach, but you won't see many whole clams. Clams stay buried under the sand and stretch their long muscular tubes, called "siphons," up to the surface. When the tide is in, they draw in water through one side of their siphons and push it out through the other side. They feed off the plankton in the water. When the tide is out, the siphons are still at the surface. But when someone steps too close to a buried clam, the clam will yank back the siphon, sending up a squirt of water.

Littleneck Clam

A clam squirted me!

Date/Time: _____ **Location:** _____

I found lots of clamshells!

Date/Time: _____ **Location:** _____

How many kinds did you find?_____

How big was the biggest?   **How big was the smallest?**

Width: _____ **Width:** _____

Length: _____ **Length:** _____

Draw some of the shells you find. You might try and identify them later using a field guide.

Moon snails tunnel under the sand to hunt clams. When a moon snail catches a clam, it wraps its foot around it. Then it uses its toothed tongue to scrape a neat round hole in the clam's shell, sticks its mouth and tongue through the hole, and eats every soft bit of the clam.

I found a clamshell with a hole punched in it!

Date/Time: _____ **Location:** _____

How wide was the hole in diameter?_____

I found a moon snail shell!

Date/Time: _____ **Location:** _____

Measure it. Width: _____ **Height:** _____ **Width of opening:** _____

Draw it.

Lewis's Moon Snail

Moon snails lay their eggs in sand collars, which look like a C-shaped piece of rubber mixed with sand.

I found a sand collar!

Date/Time: _____ **Location:** _____

Measure it. Diameter: _____

Draw it.

Sand Collar

Gulls and crows can catch clams that are just under the surface of the sand, but they can't get through their shells. To do that, they fly high above a hard rock and drop the clam to break the shells on it. Beaches where there are clams to break are fun places to watch birds. You can often see them trying to steal food from each other.

I observed a bird breaking a clam against a hard rock!

Date/Time: _____ **Location:** _____

Was it a crow or a gull?_____

How many tries did it take to break the clam?_____

What else did you observe?_____

_____

_____

_____

Gull

Even when there are no birds dropping clams, you can still find the rocks they use to try to break them open. They will be surrounded by broken clamshells.

I found a rock used for breaking clamshells!

Date/Time: _____ **Location:** _____

Notes and Sketches

Sand dollars live in the sand and keep some sand in their bodies to weigh them down so the water doesn't wash them away. When they are alive, they are black or purple and covered with tiny spines. When they are dead, they are smooth and are white or gray.

Sand Dollar

I found a live sand dollar!

Date/Time: _____ **Location:** _____

Measure it. Diameter at widest point: _____

I found a dead sand dollar!

Date/Time: _____ **Location:** _____

Measure it. Diameter at widest point: _____

Notes and Sketches

The wet sand of a beach at low tide is a great place to look for tracks.

I found tracks!

Date/Time: _____   **Location:** _____

How many toes are there?_____

Do the tracks show claws or nails or hooves?_____

Try to identify what animals left the tracks. What animals do you think have been on the beach?_____

_____

_____

_____

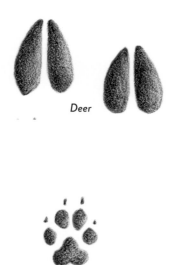

Deer

Gull

Canada Goose

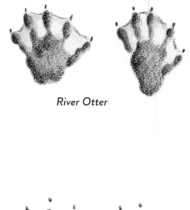

River Otter

Dog

Great Blue Heron

Crow

Racoon

Use this space to record tracks that you find.

Great blue herons spend a lot of time standing still, watching the water. You can find them near freshwater as well as on beaches. When a fish swims close enough, the heron will throw its head forward and try to grab the fish in its beak.

I saw a great blue heron!

Date/Time: _____ **Location:** _____

What did you see the heron do?_____

_____

_____

_____

_____

_____

Great Blue Heron

Draw it. Be very careful to stay quiet and still, so the heron doesn't fly away.

When you visit a beach at low tide, look for tide pools. Tide pools are home to many plants and animals. Be sure to check in corners and narrow spaces between rocks.

I found a tide pool!

Date/Time: _____ **Location:** _____

Draw a rough map of the tide pool and label it where you found interesting things.

If you touch a hermit crab, it will pop into its shell and block the entrance with its big left claw. If you leave it alone and wait awhile, its legs, eyes, and long antennae will come out again.

I found a hermit crab!

Blueband Hermit Crab

Date/Time: _____ **Location:** _____

How many kinds of shells did you notice that hermit crabs use? _____

What did you observe about their behavior? _____

_____

_____

_____

_____

Notes and Sketches

When you find them in tide pools, tube worms look like bright-colored feathers. If you touch them, they'll pull their tentacles back into their tubular shells.

I saw a tube worm!

Red Tube Worm

Date/Time: _____ **Location:** _____

Measure it. Length of the tube: _____ **Width of the opening:** _____

What did it feel like to touch one? _____

How long did it take for the tentacles to fan back out after a touch? _____

_____

_____

Notes and Sketches

Limpets hold tight to rocks using a muscular foot. A limpet's foot can cling to a rock so tightly that if you tug on it, you are more likely to break the limpet's shell than loosen the foot's grip on the rock. So be gentle.

Mask Limpet

I found limpets!

Date/Time: _____ **Location:** _____

Measure it. Length of the biggest limpet you found: _____

Length of the smallest: _____

Were all the shells the same shape or different?_____

Draw the shapes of the limpet shells you found.

Periwinkles are tiny snails that live on the highest parts of the beach. They spend most of their lives glued to rocks, sealed in their shells.

I found periwinkles!

Common Periwinkle

Date/Time: _____ **Location:** _____

Measure it. Length of shell: _____

Experiment to try with periwinkles: Put some in a bucket of seawater and time how long it takes for them to open. Then leave the bucket alone in a cool place and check on the bucket every couple of hours. If you leave them in the bucket too long, they'll crawl out and dry themselves out again.

Notes and Sketches

Rockweed, or fucus, lives high up on the beach. It has a holdfast that keeps it attached to a rock. Its leaves, or blades, have balloons that help the seaweed float upward when the tide is in.

I found fucus!

Date/Time: _____ **Location:** _____

Describe the texture of the different parts of the plant. _____

_____

_____

_____

Pop one of the floats and peel it open. What does it look like on the inside?

_____

_____

Measure it. What is the length from the holdfast to the tip of a blade?

_____

Draw it.

Rockweed

Aggregating anemones are green because plants called "algae" live inside them. You can find them on rocks at low tide or in tide pools on the beach. Go ahead and touch them, but wet your hands in seawater first and be gentle.

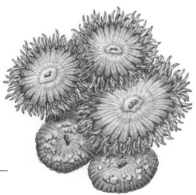

Aggregating Anemones

I found anemones!

Date/Time: _____ **Location:** _____

What did the tentacles feel like?_____

What did the anemone do when you touched it?_____

_____

How long did it take the anemone to return to the way it appeared before you touched it?_____

If you also found anemones out of water, describe how they were different from anemones in water._____

_____

_____

Notes and Sketches

Barnacles live inside crusty shells, with their heads glued to rocks. When the tide comes in, they open a door at the top of their shells, stretch out their legs, or cirri, and use them to grab tiny living things that float in the water. One type of barnacle, called a "gooseneck barnacle," lives in places that get heavy surf, such as the Pacific Ocean and the Strait of Juan de Fuca. Gooseneck barnacles have leathery, flexible necks that move when waves hit the barnacles.

When you are walking along the beach and your shadow passes over a rock covered in barnacles, the barnacles will tighten the doors of their shells, so it will sound like the rock is whispering.

Acorn Barnacle

I heard a whispering rock!

Date/Time: _____ **Location:** _____

I saw barnacles feeding!

Date/Time: _____ **Location:** _____

CHALLENGE: Draw what you saw.

Gooseneck Barnacle

If you look under rocks far down on the beach, you might find a really weird fish. The northern clingfish hangs on to the underside of rocks using a big suction cup on its belly. Be very gentle if you touch one of these fish, and always rinse your hands with seawater first.

I found a northern clingfish!

Date/Time: _____ **Location:** _____

What did you observe about it?_____

_____

_____

_____

Did it make a sound?_____

Notes and Sketches

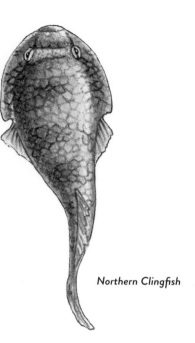

Northern Clingfish

Purple sea stars will cling to rocks in sheltered places near the bottom of the beach. If you look further down the beach, particularly in areas far from cities, you might find other kinds of sea stars, such as leather stars (which smell of garlic) or the skinny, bright red forms of blood stars. Small gray six-rayed sea stars hide under rocks. Always be gentle. Never pry a sea star off a rock.

Purple Sea Star

I found sea stars!

Date/Time: _____ **Location:** _____

How many did you find?_____

What colors were they?_____

_____

How many arms did they have?_____

What did they feel like to touch? Remember to rinse your hands in seawater before handling these animals._____

What kinds did you find? (Check a field guide.)_____

_____

_____

_____

Other observations:_____

_____

_____

_____

_____

_____

Use this space for more sketches and observations about sea stars.

If there are rocks in the middle of the beach that are heavy enough that you need to use both hands to move them, chances are there are shore crabs clustered underneath. They stay under rocks when the tide goes out because they breathe through gills, like a fish, so they need to stay wet. If you pick up a rock to look at what is underneath, always put it back carefully.

Many of the crabs you find are too small to pinch you. If one is big enough to pinch you, you can pick it up by holding it behind the pincers on the sides of the big shell covering the main part of its body. With your fingers there, the crab can wave its claws at you, but it can't reach you.

You can tell whether a crab is male or female by looking at the belly. If there's a set of plates that look like a flat oval on one side, or an old-fashioned beehive, it's a female. Sometimes there will be tiny brown eggs tucked inside the beehive shape. If it's a male, there will be a set of plates tapered to a point, like a lighthouse.

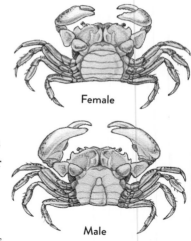

Female

Male

Purple Shore Crab

I found shore crabs!

Date/Time: _____ **Location:** _____

Measure it. Width of the body of the biggest shore crab you can find: _____

Was it a male or a female?_____

How many shore crabs did you find under a single rock?_____

Notes and Sketches

Crabs, like insects and spiders, have bodies covered in shells, which are also called "exoskeletons." When a crab grows out of its old exoskeleton, it sheds it and leaves it on the beach.

I found a crab exoskeleton!

Date/Time: _____ **Location:** _____

Measure it. Length: _____ **Width:** _____

What color was it?_____

Was the crab that shed it male or female?_____

Draw it.

Harbor seals fish in sheltered waters along the coast. They are gray or sometimes brownish with spots. You can see them from a beach when they pop up their heads to breathe and look around. If you take a ferry that crosses salt water, you can sometimes see them hauled out on rocks.

Harbor Seal

Sometimes the mother seal leaves her baby—called a "pup"—on the beach while she searches for food. If you find one, leave it alone and don't touch it. Its mother will almost certainly come back.

I saw a harbor seal!

Date/Time: _____ **Location:** _____

I saw harbor seals hauled out on rocks!

Date/Time: _____ **Location:** _____

I saw a baby harbor seal!

Date/Time: _____ **Location:** _____

What was the seal doing?_____

_____

_____

_____

You can find river otters in Puget Sound, the Salish Sea, and other sheltered waters away from the ocean, as well as lakes, ponds, and rivers. When a mother river otter is swimming with her young, called "kits," it's hard to tell how many kits there are, because they take turns diving below the water and resurfacing.

I saw a river otter!

North American River Otter

Date/Time: _____ **Location:** _____

How many were there? _____

What were they doing? _____

_____

_____

_____

Notes and Sketches

Beach pebbles come in many colors and varieties. Some were made when mud at the bottom of an old seabed turned to rocks. Others were formed in volcanoes or made under heat and pressure as the earth's crust shifted around.

Among the pebbles, you can find beach glass. Beach glass is broken glass—usually from bottles—that has been smoothed by grinding against stones. It can come in a variety of colors. White, green, and brown are the most common.

How many different kinds of rocks can you find?_____

CHALLENGE: Check a field guide. Can you identify any of them?_____

_____

_____

_____

_____

What shapes and colors are they?_____

_____

_____

_____

If you have small pebbles, try putting them in a glass jar filled with water.

How does that change how they look?_____

_____

Did you find beach glass? What colors were there?_____

_____

_____

Plastic is an increasingly common sight on our beaches and in our oceans, and it is very harmful. Animals can get tangled up in plastic can–holders or fishing line. (Fishing line is particularly deadly.) Or tiny pieces of plastic can clog animals' stomachs. When you find plastic on the beach, it's a good idea to pick it up carefully and take it away.

One important exception: if you see a syringe or a hypodermic needle on the beach, don't touch it. Tell a grown-up who can come and pick it up safely. You don't always see the point of a needle right away, so any time you see a tube of plastic on the beach with markings on it like a ruler, keep away from it.

I found plastic!

Date/Time: _____ **Location:** _____

Make a list of what you found.

CITIZEN SCIENCE: Share your observations with scientists! Check out the Marine Debris Tracker citizen science project on page 156.

The seven kinds of whales most commonly seen in our inland waters are minke whales, humpback whales, gray whales, Dall's porpoises, harbor porpoises, Pacific white-sided dolphins, and orcas.

Orcas are the most famous. There are two types of orcas that people usually see. Transient orcas stay in small groups and hunt other marine mammals, such as seals. Resident orcas can be in small groups or large pods, and eat salmon, mostly Chinook salmon. You can tell male orcas from females by looking at the fin on their back, called the "dorsal fin." Female orcas have a dorsal fin that curves toward the back, like a wing. Male orcas have a dorsal fin that is more symmetrical, like a traffic cone.

I saw orcas!

Date/Time: _____ **Location:** _____

How many did you see?_____

How many males?_____

How many females?_____

Were there babies?_____

Notes and Sketches

Orca (male)

I saw other kinds of whales!

Date/Time:_____ **Location:**_____

What kind did you think they were?_____

How many did you see?_____

Notes and Sketches

In summer protected bays are full of jellies (often called "jellyfish," though they are not fish). If you're on a ferry traveling across salt water, take a look over the side as it enters or leaves the dock, and count the jellies. You could also look from a dock, or from a beach just before high tide. When the tide goes out, you can sometimes find them stranded on the beach.

Moon Jelly

I saw jellies!

Date/Time: _____ **Location:** _____

How many did you see?_____

Draw some.

Lion's mane is a type of jelly that grows to be as big as a Frisbee, or bigger (the world record is seven feet across). It is reddish brown, and it often washes up on the beach. If you are in the water with one, stay far away. They have long tentacles that are hard to see and will give you a painful sting.

I saw a lion's mane jelly!

Date/Time: _____   **Location:** _____

Draw it.

Seawater during summer and early fall is full of plankton, including Noctiluca, a microscopic life form that glows in the dark when you stir up the water around it. When living things glow in the dark, it is called "bioluminescence." Along with Noctiluca, many jellies—also called "jellyfish"—glow in the dark. On land, some mushrooms do as well.

The best way to see Noctiluca (and maybe find a glow-in-the-dark jelly) is to go to the beach or out on a boat on a night with no moon, somewhere away from city lights. There is a lot of Noctiluca in the water from May through early October. You can create the lights yourself by stirring up the water with your hands or a paddle.

I saw Noctiluca!

Date/Time: _____ **Location:** _____

Could you see the moon?_____

Were there other lights (say, city lights or lights on ships)?_____

Weather: _____

How did you find the Noctiluca?_____

_____

_____

What did you observe?_____

_____

_____

_____

_____

_____

_____

Many water birds arrive in fall to spend the winter in sheltered bays and lakes.

Buffleheads are small black-and-white ducks that like to dive after fish. When they are in Pacific Northwest waters they tend to hang around in groups. Buffleheads have a reputation for being punctual. They'll arrive in different towns along the coast on almost the same day each year.

Bufflehead

I saw buffleheads!

Date/Time: _____ **Location:** _____

How many were there?_____

What did you observe them doing?_____

_____

_____

_____

_____

_____

CHALLENGE: Did you see other kinds of ducks on the water? Use a field guide and identify them and record what you found here._____

_____

_____

_____

_____

_____

_____

Brants are small black geese with white markings. They can be seen eating eelgrass on sandy beaches. Some of them winter in southwestern British Columbia and northwestern Washington, and others keep making their way south down the coast to Mexico.

Brant

I saw brants!

Date/Time: _____   **Location:** _____

How many were there? _____

What did you observe them doing? _____

_____

_____

_____

Notes and Sketches

CITIZEN SCIENCE: Share your observations with scientists! Check out the Christmas Bird Count citizen science project on page 155.

When big windstorms hit the coast in late fall, they clear out the kelp beds. The kelp washes up on the beach in tangled heaps.

Bull Kelp

I found kelp on the beach!

Date/Time: _____ **Location:** _____

How long was the longest piece of kelp you found? Measure it. _____

There are lots of ways to play with kelp. You can use it to decorate a sandcastle, make musical instruments out of it, or pour water through it. Record how you played with kelp. _____

_____

_____

I found other plants and animals with the kelp!

Draw some of the things you found.

Use these pages for your notes, drawings, and observations.

FRESHWATER

Two or more people can play a game called Poohsticks anywhere there is a bridge going over a stream. To play, each person finds a stick, a fir cone or pine cone, or something from nature that floats, and then goes to the upstream side of the bridge—the side the water is coming from. One person does a countdown—"5, 4, 3, 2, 1"—and at the end of the countdown everyone drops their sticks in the water. The first stick to get carried to the other side of the bridge belongs to the winner. Then everyone can play again.

What kind of floating objects made the best Poohsticks?_____

_____

_____

_____

What part of the stream had the fastest water? Draw a diagram and mark where the slow and fast parts of the stream were.

What else did you notice?_____

_____

_____

_____

When male red-winged blackbirds guard their territories near lakes, streams, marshes, or ponds, they perch somewhere high up, sing, and raise their wings and fluff their red shoulder patches, making them easier to spot. The females are harder to see, because they are a speckled brown color and often stay hidden in the brush.

I saw a red-winged blackbird!

Date/Time: _____ Location: _____

How many male red-winged blackbirds were calling?_____

How many females did you see?_____

Notes and Sketches

Red-Winged Blackbird (Male)

CITIZEN SCIENCE: Share your observations with scientists! Check out the Journey North citizen science project on page 156.

On warm days, even in winter, turtles pull themselves out of the water and sun themselves on logs. If you are near a pond on a sunny day, look for them lined up on floating logs.

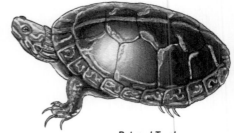

Painted Turtle

I saw turtles!

Date/Time: _____ **Location:** _____

How many turtles did you see?_____

Draw them.

In the spring black cottonwood trees release their seeds to the wind. The white fluffy seeds fly through the air. Black cottonwood trees grow near streams, rivers, and lakes.

I found cottonwood seeds!

Date/Time: _____   **Location:** _____

Try this: Gently pick up some seeds (don't crush them) and hold them above your head, then let them go. How far did they travel before they reached the ground?_____

Try it again, but this time squeeze them in your hand before you let go.

What happened?_____

_____

CHALLENGE: Look at the cottonwood seeds under a magnifying glass (or use a grown-up's phone to magnify). Draw what you found.

Cottonwood Seeds

CITIZEN SCIENCE: Share your observations with scientists! Check out the Project Budburst and PlantWatch citizen science projects on page 156.

Freshwater

Pied-billed grebes build floating nests at the side of lakes and ponds.

I found a pied-billed grebe nest!

Pied-Billed Grebe with Nest

Date/Time: _____ **Location:** _____

What were the grebes doing?_____

_____

_____

_____

_____

How many eggs did you see?_____

How many babies did you see?_____

Draw the nest.

If the nest is somewhere you go often, use this space to keep notes on what happens in the nest.

Male mallard ducks have a shiny green head, and the female is brown. They gather on ponds. In the spring females build hidden nests on the ground and sit on them until they are ready to hatch. Mallard duck babies—or ducklings—are ready to swim soon after they hatch.

Male   Female

Mallard Duck

I saw mallard ducklings!

Date/Time: _____   **Location:** _____

How many babies were there?_____

What were they doing?_____

_____

_____

How many adults were there?_____

What were the adults doing?_____

_____

_____

Notes and Sketches

Canada geese are common near cities and towns for one good reason: they love to eat grass on lawns. Any time you see a lawn convenient to a lake or a sheltered shoreline, you're likely to find a lot of goose poop around.

Canada geese have babies once a year, in the spring. After hatching, Canada goose babies—goslings—wait a day or two before they are ready to leave the nest.

I saw Canada goose goslings!

Canada Goose

Date/Time: _____   Location: _____

How many babies were there?_____

What were they doing?_____

_____

_____

How many adults were there?_____

What were they doing?_____

_____

_____

Notes and Sketches

Starting on winter nights that aren't too cold and continuing into spring, Pacific chorus frogs (also called Pacific tree frogs) gather near ponds to mate and lay eggs. You can hear the males calling for the females in the spring. Their "ribbit, ribbit, ribbit" can measure ninety decibels—as loud as a bulldozer engine.

I heard Pacific chorus frogs!

Date/Time: _____ **Location:** _____

What did they sound like?_____

What was the weather like?_____

What else did you observe?_____

_____

_____

_____

Notes and Sketches

Pacific Chorus Frog

CITIZEN SCIENCE: Share your observations with scientists! Check out the Journey North citizen science project on page 156.

The simplest way to find a frog is to scare one. Step too close to where one is sitting, and it will leap to get out of your way. But if you're ready to be still, quiet, and look carefully, you can find frogs in their hiding places. On summer days, Pacific chorus frogs often sit still on plants near the edge of ponds. If they're on a brown plant, they'll turn brown, and if they're on a green plant, they'll turn green.

I found frogs!

Date/Time: _____ **Location:** _____

How many did you find?_____

How did you find them?_____

What colors were they?_____

What were they doing?_____

_____

_____

_____

_____

_____

What else did you observe about them?_____

_____

_____

_____

_____

Dragonflies and damselflies are a lot alike. They both have long bodies and four big wings, and they both hunt other insects. You can tell a dragonfly from a damselfly when they stop flying and perch. Damselflies fold up their wings on their backs. Dragonflies hold their wings out straight.

I saw damselflies and/or dragonflies!

Date/Time: _____ **Location:** _____

How many were there?_____

What were they doing?_____

How many kinds did you see?_____

Describe them._____

_____

_____

_____

_____

Notes and Sketches

Mosaic Darner Dragonfly

Pacific Forktail Damselfly

When damselflies or dragonflies mate, the male grabs the female behind the head using claspers at the end of his abdomen while they're flying. Then they go to a quiet perch to finish mating. In some species, the male will keep hanging on to the female while she lays eggs.

I saw mating damselflies or dragonflies!

Date/Time: _____ **Location:** _____

Were they flying together?_____

Were they perching?_____

Was the female laying eggs?_____

Notes and Sketches

Dragonfly babies, or nymphs, live in freshwater. They are fierce predators.

I found a dragonfly nymph!

Date/Time: _____ **Location:** _____

Mosaic Darner Dragonfly Nymph

When a dragonfly or damselfly nymph is big enough, it will crawl out of the water, hang on to a plant, and then its exoskeleton will split at the back, and it will wriggle out in a new form, with wings. It takes a while for their big wings to unfold and harden enough for the insect to fly. Damselfly wings take about an hour, while dragonfly wings take about three hours. When they do fly away, they leave their old exoskeleton behind, still clinging to a plant. This can happen any time from spring through the fall, depending on the species, but it is most common in the summer.

I found a nymph exoskeleton!

Date/Time: _____ **Location:** _____

If you can safely get close to it, measure it. Length: _____

I found a young damselfly or dragonfly drying out!

Date/Time: _____ **Location:** _____

Draw or describe what you found.

Water striders like calm water. You can find lots of them in pools on the edge of rivers and creeks. They can skim around on the top of the water because their four back legs are covered in hairs that help them float.

Common Water Strider

I found water striders!

Date/Time: _____ **Location:** _____

Try to count them. How many did you see?_____

Pick one and watch it. As it moves around the water's surface, try and move your pencil on the paper in the same speed and direction to map its path.

Whirligig beetles live in calm freshwater. They are very tiny, and they swim around on the surface of the water, with air bubbles under their bellies keeping them afloat. They get their names from the fast way they move in tight curves and circles on the water.

I found whirligig beetles!

Date/Time: _____ **Location:** _____

Pick one whirligig beetle and as you watch it, try and move your pencil on the paper in the same speed and direction as it swims around on the water's surface.

Lily pads are the big leaves of pond lilies. The underside of the leaf stays wet and is a great hiding place for many animals. But if you put water on the top of a lily pad, it will bead up and flow right off. Try it!

Rocky Mountain Pond Lilies

I found pond lilies!

Date/Time: _____ **Location:** _____

Look under the lily pad. What animals did you see?_____

_____

_____

_____

Draw the lily pad.

Duckweed lives on the surface of calm freshwater. It's the smallest and simplest of flowering plants: just a leaf with a root dangling down. Duckweed spreads to new ponds by clinging to the legs of ducks.

I found duckweed!

Common Duckweed

Date/Time: _____ **Location:** _____

If you put your hand in water covered in duckweed and pull it out again, you should find some duckweed stuck to your hand. Try it.

What happened?_____

_____

Notes and Sketches

Beavers are most active at night, early in the morning, or late in the evening. They'll settle in wherever they find running water and trees together. You can find active lodges in some city parks. Often you won't see any beavers, but you'll hear a slap on the water as you walk up to a beaver pond. Beavers slap the water with their tails to warn other beavers that danger is approaching and it's time to hide.

American Beaver

I saw beavers!

Date/Time: _____ **Location:** _____

How many were there?_____

What were they doing?_____

_____

_____

_____

I heard a tail slap!

Date/Time: _____ **Location:** _____

Did you see any beavers?_____

What happened?_____

_____

_____

_____

While you may not see beavers, you may see lots of signs that they are around. You can see the bite marks of beavers' teeth on trees they started to cut down and on stumps where they did take the tree down. You might even spot their tracks!

I found wood that beavers chewed!

Date/Time: _____ **Location:** _____

Observations: _____

_____

I found beaver tracks!

Date/Time: _____ **Location:** _____

Draw the tracks.

American Beaver Tracks

If you go up to a pond where beavers live, you'll see their construction work in the form of a big, broad dam.

I found a beaver dam!

Date/Time: _____ **Location:** _____

About how big was it?_____

What was it made of?_____

_____

Notes and Sketches

If you visit a beaver pond, you may also find a beaver lodge, a big dome-shaped structure made out of mud and logs, at the edge of the pond, or in it, with entrances underwater.

I found a beaver lodge!

Date/Time: _____ **Location:** _____

About how big was it?_____

What was it made of?_____

_____

CHALLENGE: Draw a map of the beaver pond, labeling the dam, the lodge, and other things you observed.

Beaver Lodge

Where there's mud near a lake, pond, or river, look for animal tracks.

I found tracks!

Date/Time: _____ **Location:** _____

How many toes were there?_____

Did the tracks show claws or nails or hooves?_____

Try to identify what animals left the tracks. What animals do you think have been stopping near the water?_____

_____

_____

_____

Dog

Canada Goose

Great Blue Heron

Beaver

River Otter

Deer

Use this space to record tracks that you find.

The peak time for salmon returning to rivers—and for people going to watch salmon returning to rivers—is fall. To observe spawning salmon, find a river or creek that has salmon runs. You can often spot the salmon from the shore. If you are looking near the mouth of the creek, go around the time of high tide, because that is when most salmon go into freshwater. Most salmon runs happen the same time every year. One kind of salmon, pinks, only run in odd-numbered years.

Spawning Chum Salmon

I saw spawning salmon!

Date/Time: _____   **Location:** _____

What did it smell like?_____

Pick one fish to watch for a while. I watched a fish for _____ **minutes!**

Here's what I saw it do in that time: _____

_____

_____

_____

Draw the spawning salmon.

When salmon return to rivers, animals such as bald eagles, ravens, raccoons, and bears gather to eat them.

I saw bald eagles at a salmon stream!

Date/Time: _____ **Location:** _____

How many did you see?_____

What were they doing?_____

_____

_____

_____

Bald Eagle

Raven

I saw other animals at a salmon stream!

Date/Time: _____ **Location:** _____

What kinds of animals did you see?_____

_____

_____

_____

What were they doing?_____

_____

_____

_____

Raccoon

Use these pages for your notes, drawings, and observations.

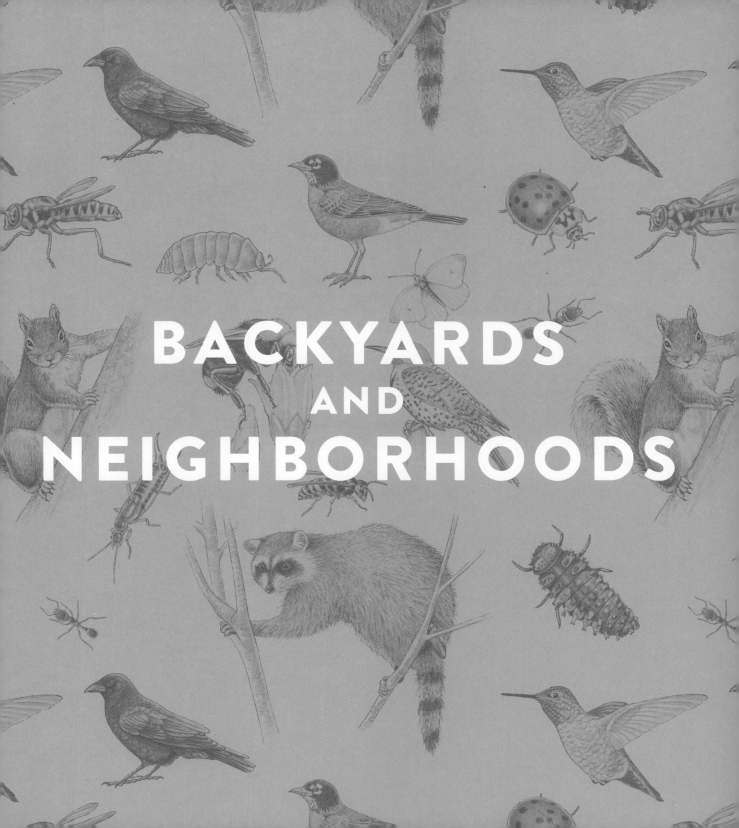

BACKYARDS
AND
NEIGHBORHOODS

Every night in late fall and winter, just before sunset, crows fly away from city neighborhoods to their night roosts. Sometimes they'll stop and gather at a wooded spot before continuing on the rest of their journey. If you see one of these flocks, watch and listen.

I watched a flock of crows on their way to a night roost!

American Crow

Date/Time: _____ Location: _____

What did you observe about how the crows behaved?_____

_____

_____

_____

How much noise did they make while they were flying?_____

How much noise did they make when they were resting?_____

CHALLENGE: What direction were they going? (To figure this out you can use a compass or a compass app on a phone.)_____

Notes and Sketches

Here's a sign that an owl or another bird of prey is around. Groups of crows and sometimes jays will gather around an owl or hawk and make lots of noise. This is called "mobbing." Some of the crows will fly above the owl or hawk, and then swoop down at it, sometimes hitting it. They will also do this to raccoons.

I saw a mobbing!

Date/Time: _____ **Location:** _____

What kinds of birds were there? (Check a field guide.)_____

_____

_____

How many did you count?_____

What animal were they mobbing?_____

Notes and Sketches

If you want to try and attract more birds to your yard, try installing a feeder or a birdbath.

If you want to figure out what kind of birds you are seeing, use a field guide. Remember to write down the date and time you see them.

What parts of your yard do different birds like and why do you think they like it?_____

_____

_____

_____

_____

_____

_____

_____

_____

Black-Capped Chickadee

CITIZEN SCIENCE: Share your observations with scientists! Check out the Project FeederWatch citizen science project on page 156.

Use this page to keep track of the birds that come to your yard.

When eastern gray squirrels are ready to mate, the female will call out in a squeaky voice, and males will chase her up and down and through trees. This can happen in summer or winter.

Eastern Gray Squirrel

I watched a squirrel mating chase!

Date/Time: _____ **Location:** _____

What caused you to notice the mating chase?_____

What did it sound like?_____

How many squirrels were involved?_____

Describe what happened._____

_____

_____

_____

_____

Notes and Sketches

When there are no leaves on the trees, it is easier to see nests. Eastern gray squirrel nests look like giant balls of twigs in the tree. Robin nests are cup-shaped and are usually in among the branches, no more that twenty-five feet off the ground. Crow nests are bigger and more untidy, and they are usually near the tops of trees.

I found a nest!

Date/Time: _____   **Location:** _____

What animal do you think the nest belongs to?_____

What did the nest look like?_____

Draw the nest.

The best time to look for tracks made by the animals around you is when it snows. Sometimes you can also find them in the mud after heavy rain, or after a heavy frost.

I found tracks!

Date/Time: _____ **Location:** _____

How many toes were there?_____

Did the tracks show claws or nails or hooves?_____

Where do you think the animal was going?_____

What animal do you think made the tracks?_____

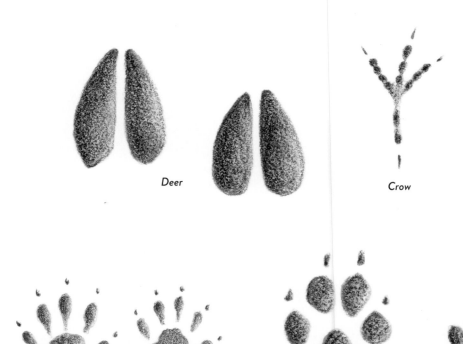

Deer

Crow

Raccoon

Dog

Cat

Use this space to record tracks that you find.

At the end of winter birds sing more often. The male birds make most of the noise. They sing to attract females and to warn other males to stay away. One of the first birds you hear is the northern flicker. It doesn't just sing; it also likes to drum. You can often find one drumming on metal chimneys or other items that make a loud noise.

I found a northern flicker!

Date/Time: _____ **Location:** _____

What was it doing?_____

_____

_____

_____

What did it sound like?_____

Notes and Sketches

Northern Flicker

Male robins start singing near the end of winter. Robins are one of the first birds to sing in the morning and the last to sing at night.

I found a robin!

Date/Time: _____   **Location:** _____

What was it doing?_____

_____

_____

_____

What sounds did it make?_____

Notes and Sketches

American Robin

CITIZEN SCIENCE: Share your observations with scientists! Check out the Journey North citizen science project on page 156.

Backyards and Neighborhoods

The first bumblebees you see every year are queen bees. They spend the winter in burrows in the ground. When they emerge, they eat and make a hive where they can lay eggs. They look after their babies, called "larvae." The larvae grow to become bumblebees that will look after the queen, who will lay more eggs.

I saw a bumblebee!

Date/Time: _____ **Location:** _____

What was it doing?_____

_____

_____

_____

Where was it going?_____

Notes and Sketches

Bumblebee

CITIZEN SCIENCE: Share your observations with scientists! Check out the Bumble Bee Watch citizen science project on page 156.

Cabbage white butterflies are one of the first butterflies to show up in the spring. They like to lay eggs on plants that are in the mustard family, such as cabbage and kale.

I saw a cabbage white butterfly!

Cabbage White Butterfly

Date/Time: _____   **Location:** _____

What was it flying near?_____

Did it land on any plants?_____

What plants were they?_____

_____

Notes and Sketches

CITIZEN SCIENCE: Share your observations with scientists! Check out the eButterfly citizen science project on page 156.

On warm, dry days in the spring you can sometimes see brown patches near cracks in the pavement. Look closely, and these brown patches are swarms of pavement ants.

I found a pavement ant swarm!

Date/Time: _____ **Location:** _____

Draw the swarm. Label places where the ants were coming in and out of the

pavement.

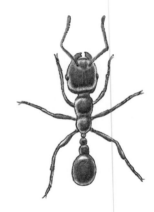

Pavement Ant

Pavement Ant Swarm

Ladybugs lay their eggs under leaves and in places where there are likely to be a lot of tiny insects, such as aphids, that they like to eat. Their eggs hatch into spiky black larvae, which eat until they are big enough to change into their adult form.

Ladybug

I found ladybug larvae!

Date/Time: _____   **Location:** _____

How many?_____   **Measure them. Length:** _____

I found an adult ladybug!

Date/Time: _____   **Location:** _____

What was it doing?_____

_____

_____

_____

_____

How many spots did it have?_____

Ladybug Larva

CITIZEN SCIENCE: Share your observations with scientists!
Check out the Lost Ladybug Project on page 156.

Bushtits are tiny gray birds that build amazing nests. Male and female bushtits work together to weave a nest out of spiderwebs, grasses, and bits of plants. It dangles from a branch, looking like a fuzzy green sock.

I found a bushtit nest!

Date/Time: _____   **Location:** _____

What did you see the bushtits doing? _____

_____

_____

_____

What did you hear? _____

Draw the nest.

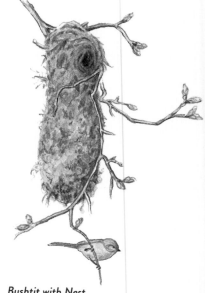

Bushtit with Nest

If the nest is somewhere you go often, use this space to write down what you observe each time you visit.

If you see a patch of white foam on a twig near the ground in the springtime or early summer, there's a spittlebug inside. It is actually the baby—or nymph—of an insect called a "froghopper." And the foam isn't spit. It's pee, mixed with air and some sticky stuff. A spittlebug will pee more than a hundred times its body weight every day.

While the spittlebug is growing, it will stick its rear end out of the foam to breathe. When it is ready to change into a froghopper, it will go into a big bubble and change, and will pee less so the foam will dry away.

Spittlebug Foam

I found spittlebug foam!

Date/Time: _____ **Location:** _____

Measure it. Length: _____ **Width:** _____

Are there more patches of foam around? How many? _____

Can you see the nymph? _____

CHALLENGE: Very gently move the foam away from one spittlebug and draw what you find. You might need to use a magnifying glass or magnify what you see using a phone.

If the spittlebug is in a place you go often, take notes here on how it changes.

Barn swallows spend the winter in Central and South America. They come back to the Pacific Northwest in April and swoop around, eating insects. Males and females work together to build cup-shaped nests out of mud. They like to use places like the spot where the roof of a building hangs over the wall.

I saw swallows!

Date/Time: _____ **Location:** _____

What were they doing?_____

_____

_____

_____

How many swallows did you count?_____

Barn Swallow

While young swallows are in the nest, their parents fly back and forth. They bring their babies food, and they take away their babies' poop and drop it away from the nest.

I saw a barn swallow nest!

Date/Time: _____ **Location:** _____

How many nests did you see in the area? What do you see in the nest?

_____

_____

Did you see an adult swallow fly up to the nest? What happened?

_____

_____

_____

Barn Swallow Nest

If the nest is somewhere you go often, use this space to take notes about what you observed each time you visited.

CITIZEN SCIENCE: Share your observations with scientists! Check out the Journey North citizen science project on page 156.

Pill bugs have seven pairs of legs, making a total of fourteen. They also have two pairs of antennae, one big and one small, for a total of four. Their back has seven plates.

Pill Bug

I found pill bugs!

Date/Time: _____ **Location:** _____

How many were there?_____

What sizes were they?_____

_____

Draw one.

You can find earwigs in damp, shady places, such as under a piece of loose bark. You can tell males from females by looking at the pincers on their abdomens: females have straight pincers; males have curved pincers.

Female

Male

European Earwig

I found earwigs!

Date/Time: _____ **Location:** _____

How many were there?_____

How many are males?_____ **How many are females?**_____

What sizes were they?_____

What did you observe about them?_____

_____

_____

_____

Notes and Sketches

Find a spot in your yard to dig. What did you find?

Use these two pages to draw and write notes about what you found.

Try sitting and observing different kinds of flowers and recording what animals come by to drink the nectar and spread pollen. Animals that help plants this way are called "pollinators." Examples of pollinators are butterflies, bees, wasps, flies, and hummingbirds.

Here are some great nectar plants to observe: wild roses, bee balm, lavender, daisies, and sunflowers.

When you have finished observing one kind of flower, try a different kind.

Use this space to record your observations. As you're observing, determine if different flowers attract different pollinators.

TYPE OF FLOWER:

Date/Time: _____ **Location:** _____

Pollinators seen: _____

_____

TYPE OF FLOWER:

Date/Time: _____ **Location:** _____

Pollinators seen: _____

_____

TYPE OF FLOWER:

Date/Time: _____ **Location:** _____

Pollinators seen: _____

_____

TYPE OF FLOWER:

Date/Time: _____ **Location:** _____

Pollinators seen: _____

_____

Notes and Sketches

Western tiger swallowtails are big yellow and black butterflies. People often see them near freshwater because when they are in their caterpillar form, they eat leaves of trees that thrive near streams, ponds, and lakes, such as willows and cottonwoods. You might see one sipping nectar from a flower.

I saw a western tiger swallowtail!

Date/Time: _____ **Location:** _____

What was it doing?_____

_____

_____

_____

If you know what kind of plants were nearby (or can identify them in a

field guide), write them down._____

_____

_____

Notes and Sketches

Western Tiger Swallowtail

Some years painted lady butterflies can be found wherever daisies or thistles, the plants that make their favorite nectar, grow. Other years painted ladies are rare. The butterflies spend the winter in the deserts of the American Southwest and northern Mexico, and then migrate north in the spring and summer. But they don't make the whole journey every year. Scientists are figuring out why. One factor is how much it rains in the desert in winter. If it rains a lot, flowers bloom while the butterflies are there. This helps the butterflies thrive, which means more painted ladies head north in the spring.

Painted Lady Butterfly

I found a painted lady!

Date/Time: _____   **Location:** _____

If you know what kind of plants were nearby (or can identify them in a

field guide), write them down._____

_____

_____

What was it doing?_____

_____

_____

_____

CITIZEN SCIENCE: Share your observations with scientists!
Check out the eButterfly citizen science project on page 156.

Anna's hummingbirds are fun to watch. They come to feeders and hover, drinking sugar water, using their long tongues. You can also see them at flowers (fireweed is a favorite). One might even come up to you if you sit still and wear a red shirt. If there's more than one hummingbird around, they're often battling.

Colorful full-grown males, the ones with the big shiny patches, will chase away the less flashy females and juveniles. The females and juveniles will find places to perch and sneak trips to bird feeders and flower patches when the big males aren't looking.

Anna's Hummingbird

I observed hummingbirds!

Date/Time: _____ **Location:** _____

How many did you see?_____

What were they doing?_____

_____

_____

_____

Notes and Sketches

Male Anna's hummingbirds do flight displays. They are showing off for female hummingbirds and warning other males to stay away from their territories. The tiny bird will fly up to 130 feet high—a height that is about as tall as three-and-a-half telephone poles—and then dive down toward the ground, swooping up at the end of the dive while making a chirping noise through his tail feathers.

I saw a hummingbird mating display!

Date/Time: _____ **Location:** _____

How many times did the hummingbird dive?_____

Did you see other hummingbirds around?_____

What else happened?_____

_____

_____

_____

CHALLENGE: Can you draw the hummingbird's flight path?

By the beginning of summer, raccoon babies start following their mothers out of their den. You are more likely to see them in the early morning, in the evening, or at night, which is when raccoons are most active.

I saw raccoons!

Date/Time: _____ **Location:** _____

How many? _____

_____

_____

_____

What were they doing? _____

Notes and Sketches

Raccoon

By the end of summer yellow jackets are plentiful. Some make paper nests in high places, such as trees. Others nest in holes in trees or in burrows underground. When you are walking around off trail in a wild area during the summer, it's important to look where you step in case there is a wasp nest there. (Other tips to avoid being stung: Stay calm. Don't swat at wasps, even if they land on you. Put food and garbage away.)

Yellow Jacket

Late summer is also a time when people like to eat picnics, and wasps like to steal their food. Wasps like some food more than others. (If you're drinking out of cans or bottles, always pour your drink into cups so you can see if a wasp landed in your beverage.)

Wasps came to my picnic!

Date/Time: _____ **Location:** _____

What food or drinks were they interested in?_____

_____

_____

I found a wasp nest! (Don't go too close!)

Date/Time: _____ **Location:** _____

What did you observe about it?_____

_____

_____

_____

After fog or a light rain it is easy to see spiderwebs, because droplets collect on the webs. Go out in your yard on a morning when it is easy to see spiderwebs.

I found spiderwebs!

Date/Time: _____ **Location:** _____

How many spiderwebs did you find?_____

How many different kinds of spiderwebs did you see?_____

What did you see caught in the webs?_____

_____

_____

Did you see any spiders?_____

How many different kinds of spiders did you see?_____

Notes and Sketches

Orb weavers build big flat webs with a spiral of silk like spokes on a wheel. The best time to find spiders building webs is the morning after a heavy rainstorm.

I watched an orb weaver build a web!

Date/Time: _____ **Location:** _____

Draw what happened at each stage.

Orb Weaver with Web

Use these pages for your notes, drawings, and observations.

EXPLORE MORE!

Participate in Citizen Science Projects

Citizen science is when people who are not professional scientists collect information that helps science. There are so many citizen science projects going on in our communities, and quite a few are great for kids. Here are some good places to get involved.

General

iNaturalist (iNaturalist.org). The California Academy of Scientists and the National Geographic Society maintain this online community, which includes observations from more than three million people worldwide. Add your observations or join projects.

Project Noah (ProjectNoah.org) is a place where you can post pictures of living things you find, and experts on the internet can identify them. You can join what the site calls "Missions," collecting data about particular things, such as moths or ladybugs. Also check out Project Noah Nature School.

SciStarter (SciStarter.org) has a directory of local and wide-scale projects all over the world, and you can easily search for projects suitable for kids.

Birds

Christmas Bird Count (www.audubon.org/conservation/join -christmas-bird-count). Groups around North America do big bird counts on different dates in December. Go on the website, find a group near you doing a count, and join a team. It's OK if you are a beginner. (There will be experienced birders on your team.)

Great Backyard Bird Count (BirdCount.org). Each February people of all ages from around the world come together to participate by watching and counting birds using eBird, one of the world's largest nature databases.

Journey North (JourneyNorth.org) collects volunteer observations from around North America about several animals including robins, earthworms, red-winged blackbirds, frogs, and barn swallows.

Project FeederWatch (FeederWatch.org). The Cornell Laboratory of Ornithology and Birds Canada run this project. From November to April, people count the birds that come to their yards. You don't need to have a feeder.

Insects

Bumble Bee Watch (BumbleBeeWatch.org) tracks different species of bumblebees around North America. Take a picture of a bumblebee and upload it to the Bumble Bee Watch website. Use the information on the site to identify it (an expert will check to see if you are correct).

eButterfly (e-Butterfly.org) collects photos and observations about butterflies from around North America. Even if you can't identify the butterfly you saw, you can enter it.

Lost Ladybug Project (www.LostLadybug.org). Entomologists are trying to track the populations of different kinds of ladybugs around North America. To help them out, take pictures of a ladybug and send in the picture, along with a form with the time, date, location and habitat.

Plants

Project Budburst (Budburst.org) collects observations about plants in the United States and what time of year they grow, bloom, make fruits, or shed seeds. It helps scientists track whether plants are changing the timing of how they grow year to year in different places. If you're in Canada, you can participate in **PlantWatch** (NatureWatch.ca/PlantWatch).

Plastics

Marine Debris Tracker (DebrisTracker.org) tracks litter all over the world. You can use an app to report the kinds of garbage you find and where you find it. When volunteers do this, it can help scientists trace how plastic garbage moves to different places.

Field Guides to Check Out

Here's a list of useful field guides that kids often like. Some are meant for kids or adult beginners. Others are books that even experts would reach for.

General

Curious Kids Nature Guide: Explore the Amazing Outdoors of the Pacific Northwest by Fiona Cohen (author) and Marni Fylling (illustrator)

Amphibians

Amphibians of the Pacific Northwest edited by Lawrence L. C. Jones, William P. Leonard, and Deanna H. Olson

Birds

Birds of Seattle and Puget Sound by Chris Fisher
Look at that Bird! A Young Naturalist's Guide to Pacific Northwest Birding by Karen DeWitz
Stokes Beginner's Guide to Birds: Western Region by Donald and Lillian Stokes

Insects

Bugs of Washington and Oregon or *Bugs of British Columbia* by John Acorn (author) and Ian Sheldon (illustrator)
Field Guide to Insects of North America by Eric R. Eaton and Kenn Kaufman
A Field Guide to Insects of the Pacific Northwest by Dr. Robert Cannings
Pacific Northwest Insects by Merrill A. Peterson

Mammals and Tracks

Wildlife of the Pacific Northwest by David Moskowitz

Marine Life

Fylling's Illustrated Guide to Pacific Coast Tide Pools by Marni Fylling
The New Beachcomber's Guide to the Pacific Northwest by J. Duane Sept

Plants

Plants of the Pacific Northwest Coast or *Plants of Coastal British Columbia* by Jim Pojar and Andy MacKinnon

Rocks

A Field Guide to the Identification of Pebbles by Eileen Van der Flier-Keller

Rocks, Minerals, and Geology of the Pacific Northwest by Leslie Moclock and Jacob Selander

Museums and Nature Centers to Visit

There are lots of wonderful museums and nature centers to visit in the Pacific Northwest! Here are some great ones, where you can look at exhibits and bring your questions to experts.

Oregon

BEAVERTON: Tualatin Hills Nature Center

BEND: High Desert Museum

CAVE JUNCTION: Rusk Ranch Nature Center

COOS BAY: South Slough National Estuarine Research Reserve

THE DALLES: Columbia Gorge Discovery Center and Museum

DEPOE BAY: Whale Watching Center

EUGENE: University of Oregon Museum of Natural and Cultural History

HILLSBORO: Jackson Bottom Wetlands Preserve Nature Center

NEWPORT: Hatfield Marine Science Center, Oregon Coast Aquarium

PORTLAND: Tryon Creek State Natural Area Nature Center, World Forestry Center Discovery Museum

REEDSPORT: Umpqua Discovery Center

SEASIDE: Seaside Aquarium

SHERWOOD: Tualatin River National Wildlife Refuge Visitor Center

SUNRIVER: Sunriver Nature Center & Observatory

TILLAMOOK: Tillamook Forest Center

Washington

BELLINGHAM: Marine Life Center

COULEE CITY: Dry Falls Visitor Center

DES MOINES: Marine Science and Technology Center

EVERETT: Adopt a Stream Foundation and Northwest Stream Center

FRIDAY HARBOR: The Whale Museum

ISSAQUAH: Issaquah State Salmon Hatchery

LANGLEY: Langley Whale Center

NORTH BEND: Cedar River Watershed Education Center

OCEAN SHORES: Coastal Interpretive Center

OLYMPIA: Billy Frank Jr. Nisqually National Wildlife Refuge
Visitor Center, Puget Sound Estuarium

PORT ANGELES: Feiro Marine Life Center

POULSBO: SEA Discovery Center

RICHLAND: The REACH Museum

SEATTLE: Burke Museum of History and Culture

TACOMA: Tacoma Nature Center

British Columbia

CHILLIWACK: Great Blue Heron Nature Reserve

COURTENAY: Courtenay and District Museum and Paleontology Centre

COWICHAN BAY: Cowichan Estuary Nature Centre

DELTA: George C. Reifel Migratory Bird Sanctuary

MADEIRA PARK: Iris Griffith Field Studies & Interpretive Centre

NORTH VANCOUVER: Lynn Canyon Ecology Centre, Capilano
River Hatchery

OSOYOOS: Osoyoos Desert Centre

RICHMOND: Richmond Nature Park

SIDNEY: Sidney Museum

SURREY: Surrey Nature Centre

UCLUELET: Ucluelet Aquarium

VANCOUVER: Stanley Park Nature House, Beaty Biodiversity Museum

VERNON: Allan Brooks Nature Centre

VICTORIA: Royal British Columbia Museum

Explore More!

INDEX

ABOUT THE AUTHOR AND ILLUSTRATOR

FIONA COHEN grew up in Victoria, BC, and now lives in Seattle, Washington. She enjoys exploring the natural world, growing vegetables, and hiking. Her favorite bird is the American dipper.

A science illustrator, writer, and educator, **MARNI FYLLING** has a BS in zoology from UC Davis and a graduate certificate in natural science illustration from UC Santa Cruz. Her favorite thing to do is explore tide pools—although sketching insects and wildflowers (or just about anything else) is a close second. She is the author and illustrator of *Fylling's Illustrated Guide to Pacific Coast Tide Pools* and *Fylling's Illustrated Guide to Nature in Your Neighborhood.*

ALSO AVAILABLE

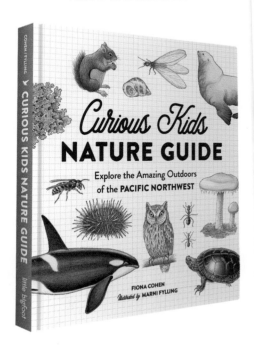